Date: 01/26/12

Volcano Alert!

Paul Challen

Crabtree Publishing Company
www.crabtreebooks.com

DISASTER ALERT!

presented by:

Crabtree Publishing Company

www.crabtreebooks.com

PMB 16A, 350 Fifth Avenue,
Suite 3308,
New York, NY 10118

612 Welland Avenue,
St. Catharines,
Ontario, Canada
L2M 5V6

73 Lime Walk,
Headington,
Oxford, 0X3 7AD
United Kingdom

For Sam, Evelina, and Henry

Coordinating editor: Ellen Rodger

Copy editors: Sean Charlebois, Carrie Gleason

Designer and production coordinator: Rosie Gowsell

Proofreader: Adrianna Morganelli

Art director: Rob MacGregor

Indexer: Wendy Scavuzzo

Photo research: Allison Napier

Prepress: Embassy Graphics

Printing: Worzalla Publishing Company

Consultant: Dr. Richard Cheel, Earth Sciences Department, Brock University

Photographs: AFP/CORBIS: p. 7 (middle); Bettmann/CORBIS: p. 22 (top), p. 25 (top); Jeremy Bishop/Photo Researchers Inc.: cover; Jeremy Bishop/SCIENCE PHOTO LIBRARY: p. 19 (top); Philippe Bourseiller/Photo Researchers, Inc.: p. 22 (bottom); Private Collection/Bridgeman Art Library: p. 5 (bottom); Richard A. Cooke/CORBIS: p. 10 (top); CORBIS: p. 10 (bottom), p. 11 (bottom), p. 27 (left); Tony Craddock/SCIENCE PHOTO LIBRARY: p. 5 (top); Jacque Durieux/Photo Researchers, Inc.: p. 23 (top); B. Edmaier/Photo Researchers, Inc.: title page; Bernhard Edmaier/SCIENCE PHOTO LIBRARY: p. 17 (bottom), p. 29 (top right); David Hardy/SCIENCE PHOTO LIBRARY: p. 18 (top); The Illustrated London News Picture Library, London, UK/Bridgeman Art Library: p. 20; Krafft/Photo Researchers, Inc.: p. 13 (bottom), p. 21 (top and middle right); John Lund/Getty Images: p. 4 (top); O. Louis Mazzatenta/Getty Images: p. 3; David Muench/CORBIS: p. 7 (bottom); National Oceanic and Atmospheric Administration/Department of Commerce: p. 15 (top); Novosti Press Agency/Photo Researchers, Inc.: p. 16 (bottom); Phillips/Bridgeman Art Library: p. 21 (left); PhotoLink/Getty Images: p. 29 (left); Roger Ressmeyer/CORBIS: p. 4 (bottom), p. 11 (top), p. 16 (top), p. 24 (bottom), p. 26, p. 27 (right); Pete Turner/Getty Images: p. 24 (top), p. 28, p. 29 (bottom); Pierre Vauthey/CORBIS SYGMA: p. 23 (bottom)

Maps: Jim Chernishenko: p. 8, p. 9

Illustrations: Robert MacGregor: p. 12; Dan Pressman: pp. 6-7, p. 13 (top, middle), pp. 14-15, p. 17 (top), p. 18 (all); David Wysotski: pp. 30-31

Cover: A Volcanologist in a protective suit, stands in front of a volcano.

Contents: A skeleton preserved by ash from the eruption of Mount Vesuvius in 79 A.D.

Title page: Volcanoes sometimes erupt in a fiery show of lava.

Published by
Crabtree Publishing Company

Copyright © 2004

Cataloging-in-Publication Data

Challen, Paul C. (Paul Clarence), 1967-
Volcano alert! / Paul Challen.
p. cm. -- (Disaster alert!)
Includes index.
ISBN 0-7787-1570-1 (rlb) -- ISBN 0-7787-1602-3 (pbk.)
1. Volcanoes--Juvenile literature. 2. Seismology--Juvenile literature.
I. Title. II. Series.
QE521.3.C455 2004
551.21--dc22
2004000835
LC

Table of Contents

Sleeping Giants

All over the world, volcanoes can be found on top of the Earth's surface and on the bottom of large bodies of water. Often, these massive structures sit for many years – even centuries – without making a sound.

At other times, the story is much different. When volcanoes erupt, they cause tremendous damage. During eruptions, burning hot rocks, ash, steam, and lava shoot out of the volcano, destroying anything in their path. Violent volcanic eruptions cause great damage to property and the environment. Houses, public buildings, and even entire villages, forests, and farms are destroyed. The world's worst volcanic disasters have claimed thousands of lives and cost billions of dollars in repairs.

What is a disaster?
A disaster is a destructive event that affects the natural world and human communities. Some disasters are predictable and others occur without warning. Coping successfully with a disaster often depends on a community's preparation.

Ash and debris deposited during a volcanic eruption destroyed this house. People who live near volcanoes must be aware of the dangers.

Living in the shadow

Today, the scientists who study volcanoes, called volcanologists, know that eruptions are not caused by angry gods and goddesses who dwell underneath the Earth, but by natural forces. This knowledge helps people who live in the shadow of volcanoes to recognize when volcanoes threaten to erupt. Volcanoes can be dangerous – but they are also awe-inspiring natural wonders.

A singed sign warns of dangerous lava flows in Hawaii.

EXTREME BEYOND THIS POINT!

Collapse of lava bench occurs without warning, causing violent steam explosions and ocean surge.

1
ACTIVE LAVA BENCH
OLD LAVA
LOOSE MATERIAL
UNDERWATER TUBES

2
LOOSE MATERIAL ERODED BY OCEAN CURRENTS

Volcano myths

Ancient peoples thought volcanic eruptions were the work of angry gods, determined to punish people for deeds that displeased them. In ancient Rome, people believed that a volcano's explosion was caused by the Roman god Vulcan, who worked in a blacksmith shop under the Sicilian island of Vulcano. Vulcan made weapons for his fellow gods, and when his workshop became busy, Romans believed hot rocks and liquid metal flew up from below the Earth's surface.

Vulcan forges a volcanic eruption.

What is a Volcano?

Volcanoes that erupt regularly are known as "active" volcanoes. Ones that have not erupted for a long time are known as "dormant", and volcanoes that seem to have stopped erupting altogether are called "extinct".

Eruptions occur when gasses, molten rock, ash, and other materials are forced out from under the Earth's surface through giant cracks in the Earth's crust.

Often, magma flows through openings, called vents, and collects outside the vents to form the hill-like shape of a volcano. Sometimes, the magma erupts from the Earth. Eruptions can be very violent, and the magma, gasses, and ash expelled from a volcano are very dangerous to anything living nearby.

The layer just below the Earth's crust, called the mantle, contains magma, or molten rock. Large underground bodies of melted rock are referred to as magma chambers.

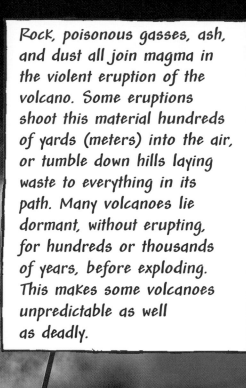

Rock, poisonous gasses, ash, and dust all join magma in the violent eruption of the volcano. Some eruptions shoot this material hundreds of yards (meters) into the air, or tumble down hills laying waste to everything in its path. Many volcanoes lie dormant, without erupting, for hundreds or thousands of years, before exploding. This makes some volcanoes unpredictable as well as deadly.

Magma moves through cracks, fissures, or vents to form volcanoes.

Shape and form

Volcanologists believe that each volcano is different. They classify volcanoes according to their appearance, and how they were formed. Magma that erupts on the surface of the Earth is called lava. Lava hardens and cools in different ways. If the lava flows for a long distance before hardening, it makes a volcano with a gradual slope to its sides, and a wide opening. The world's biggest active volcano, Mauna Loa in Hawaii, is a shield volcano.

A cinder cone volcano refers to a volcano where lava hardens quickly to form high sides and a cone-like appearance

Shield volcanoes are named because of the way they look like a soldier's shield lying face down.

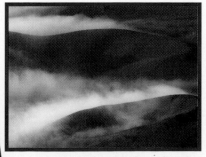

Caldera volcanoes happen when the entire top of the volcano is blown off in an explosion, leaving a huge opening.

How Volcanoes Form

Think of the Earth as it is shown on a flat map. The continents and land masses are separated by bodies of water. Looking at the Earth's surface tells us only a small part of the story of our planet. The rest of the story happens below the Earth's surface.

Millions of years ago, the Earth's land formed one big mass, known as Pangaea. Under the Earth's crust, in the mantle, are large quantities of very hot rock, called magma. As the hot magma gets stirred up by a process called **convection**, it causes the Earth's crust to crack. Cracking split Pangaea into the land masses or continents on Earth today, separated by oceans and seas. This process is known as Continental Drift.

When magma reaches the surface of the Earth, it is called lava. There are many different types of lava. Some lava bubbles up and lumps over on the Earth's surface.

Not every part of the planet has volcanoes. Volcanoes are located around the world in specific patterns. Millions of years ago, the land masses on Earth were joined. They drifted apart to form the continents as we know them today. The drifting was caused by cracks in the Earth's crust.

200 million years ago

Eurasia

North America

PANGAEA

South America

Africa

India

Australia

Antarctica

Today

North America

Asia

India

Africa

South America

Australia

Antarctica

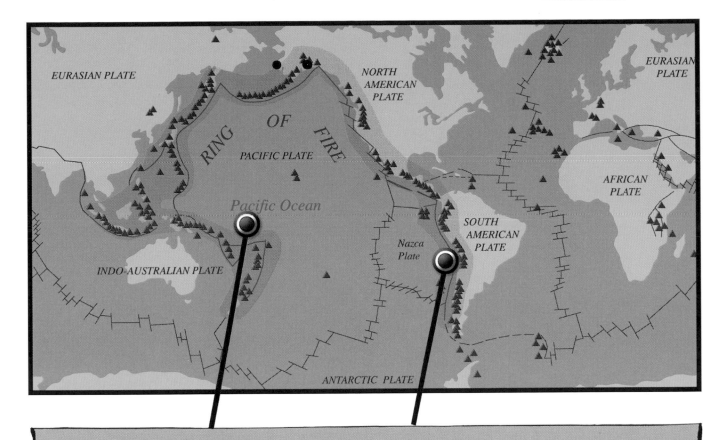

The Pacific Plate, in the Pacific Ocean, is moving slowly against the smaller plates next to it. Over time, cracks formed by these clashing plates release the tremendous heat trapped in the mantle, melting the plate's rock into magma. The magma moves upward and surges through the cracks in the crust caused by all the crashing and bumping. This forms volcanoes in a giant loop around the plate's edge, known as the Ring of Fire.

Tectonic plates

The activity under the Earth's surface is continuous. Cracks, or faults, develop when the Earth's tectonic plates – dozens of gigantic, rocky layers – push apart and slide together and over each other under the Earth's surface. This shifting underneath the surface allows magma to escape from beneath the plates. When the faults get large enough, the incredibly hot magma builds up and eventually bursts out of them. The result is a volcano.

In the zone

There are three areas in which cracks in the Earth's surface become large enough for volcanoes to form. In subduction zones, one tectonic plate slides under another. In rift zones, two tectonic plates separate from each other. In hot spots, cracks develop in the middle of the tectonic plates. The shifting of tectonic plates also affects what goes on above the Earth's surface. Vigorous shifting of the plates leads to earthquakes, or vibrations in the Earth's crust that can range in force from gentle to severe.

Residents examine the build up of rocky aa lava that has blocked a road in Hawaii. Less solid pahoehoe lava (inset) folds over the land near a volcano.

Lava

Lava is magma that has reached the surface of the Earth. There are several different types of lava. Some lava, known by its Hawaiian name of pahoehoe (pronounced pa-hoy-hoy) looks runny, and flows out of the volcano like honey from a jar. As layer upon layer of pahoehoe cools, it collects and forms shield volcanoes and flat-shaped mountains. Other lava is chunky and rough-looking, and is also called by its Hawaiian name, aa (pronounced ah-ah). This thick lava breaks into chunks as it flows along.

Depending on its thickness, lava moves at various speeds. The fastest lava flow in history was measured at almost 40 mph (60 km/h) at the Nyiragongo volcano in Zaire, Africa. Very thick lava only moves down the slopes of volcanoes at the very slow speed of a few yards (meters) per day.

This flow of lava filled a bathroom and scorched the sink.

Debris and Clouds

When volcanoes spew lava into the air, hot pieces of rock break off and fly in all directions. This debris is known as **pyroclasts**, which means "fire-broken". About 80 percent of the material expelled by a volcanic eruption is pyroclastic. Pyroclasts include small soft lumps called bombs and larger chunks called blocks. Hard, scratchy ash is also expelled with the pryoclast. The ash, or tephra, is dangerous because it falls so thickly it can smother people. Small bits of rock called lapilli or "tiny stones", are also ejected.

Thick grey pyroclastic clouds make day into night miles from the volcano they come from.

Pele's hair

In Hawaii, the Kilauea volcano produces an unusual lava known as "Pele's Hair". Pele's hair is long thin pieces of volcanic rock that look like strands of hair. Often, when Kilauea erupts, the extreme heat combines with liquid basalt to produce a glass-like lava. Hawaiians named the lava Pele's Hair, after the Hawaiian goddess of fire. Ancient Hawaiians believed Pele lived inside the Kilauea volcano and made it erupt when she was angry.

11

Busting Loose

The Earth's core, mantle, and crust contain all the ingredients needed for a fiery volcanic eruption.

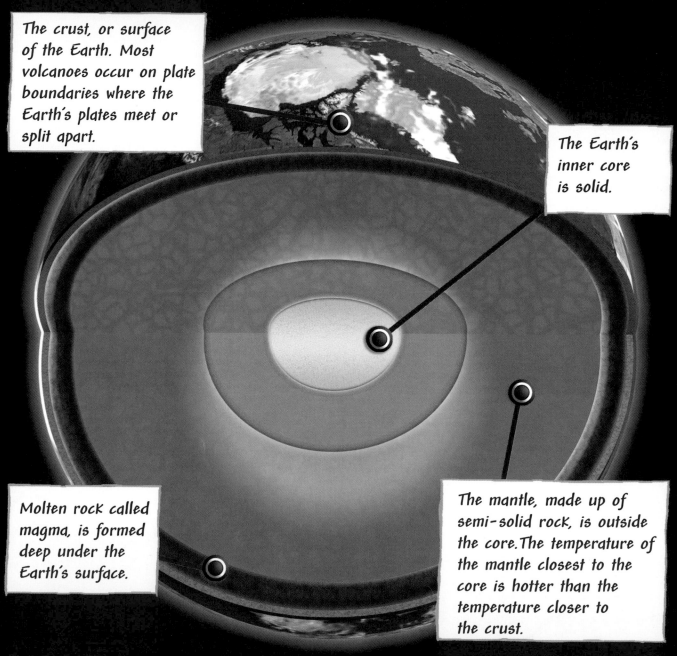

The crust, or surface of the Earth. Most volcanoes occur on plate boundaries where the Earth's plates meet or split apart.

The Earth's inner core is solid.

Molten rock called magma, is formed deep under the Earth's surface.

The mantle, made up of semi-solid rock, is outside the core. The temperature of the mantle closest to the core is hotter than the temperature closer to the crust.

An eruption

Volcanic eruptions occur when cracks in the Earth, caused by moving plates that make up the planet's crust, allow magma to emerge through the volcanic vent. Violent eruptions shoot ash and dust into the air above the volcano. Pyroclastic clouds eject above the volcano and rain down the sides. In some volcanoes, lava surges down the volcano, covering the land around it .

Divergent boundaries

At divergent boundaries or margins, plates are forced apart. The pressure forces hot magma to the surface of Earth. Most divergent boundaries are under the oceans in rift zones.

Convergent boundaries

At convergent boundaries or margins, plates move toward each other. When they meet, one plate slides beneath another in a process called subduction. Subduction usually happens where ocean plates slide under continental plates. Subduction created the **Andes Mountains** at the boundary of the Nazca Plate and the South American Plate, on the Pacific edge of South America. When two continental plates converge, the plates scrunch up to form mountains, such as the **Himalaya Mountain** range. Earthquakes at convergent boundaries begin deep in the crust and are strong and destructive.

Divergent boundary

Convergent boundary

Underwater volcano

Not all volcanoes are on land. Many volcanoes form under water in the Earth's oceans. Scientists believe that more than 90 percent of all volcanoes on Earth are located in the oceans.

Underwater lava

Volcanoes erupt differently under water. Instead of flowing down the volcano's side and away from it, lava from ocean volcanoes builds up outside the volcano's vent. The lava build-up often takes thousands of years to reach ocean surface height. Over time, the volcanoes break through to the surface and form an island.

Black smokers support an amazing variety of life deep under the sea. The animals, including sea worms, that live around black smokers are able to change the poisonous chemicals created by the black smokers into food. The smokers are located so deep under the ocean that they were not discovered until 1977.

Early eruptions

A small volcano emerges on the ocean floor. Nothing is noticeable on the ocean surface.

Volcano building

Lava builds up the volcano, increasing its size. It is still undetectable on the surface

Black smokers

Cracks on the bottom of sea and ocean floors are responsible for black smokers. Black smokers, or hydrothermal plumes, occur when ocean water seeps through cracks and travels down into the Earth's crust. There, the water meets with extreme heat, and mixes with minerals found in the Earth's mantle – such as sulfur, copper, gold, zinc, and iron. The heat causes such pressure that the water is blasted back up through **fissures**. The minerals the water transports from under the sea floor give it a black appearance.

Black smokers are up to 700° Farenheit (370° Celsius), which is hot enough to melt steel.

Surface eruption

As eruptions continue, the volcano emerges on the ocean surface.

An island is born

The volcano forms an island. Over time, vegetation grows, and birds inhabit.

15

Volcano Forecasting

As dangerous and deadly as volcanoes can be, many people have no choice but to live near them. In the past, people watched for signs or trusted their luck. Today, using information gathered by scientific instruments, volcanologists are often able to warn people living near volcanoes before an eruption actually happens.

In many countries with active volcanoes, volcanologists, attempt to get as close as possible to the vents of an active volcano to record magma levels as they rise. This information helps them to predict when the volcano will erupt. Volcanologists taking magma measurements wear special suits, which reflect heat and protect the scientists from the volcano's deadly gasses and molten rock and ash. Even experienced volcano experts are not safe from sudden explosions, and many have been killed trying to collect information.

(above, right) Volcanologists visually examine a lava dam.

(Right) Protective suits are worn by volcanologists who examine active volcanoes close-up.

Volcanologist equipment

In many parts of the world, volcanologists use sensitive equipment to predict volcanic eruptions. One piece of equipment is called a tilt meter, which measures movements on the Earth's surface. Crack meters, measure fissures, or breaks in the walls of volcanoes. Seismic sensors keep track of the earthquakes that often happen before volcanoes erupt. Volcanologists also use satellites that orbit the Earth to help predict eruptions.

Tilt meter

Mount Etna: A waiting game

Mount Etna, on the island of Sicily off the southeast coast of Italy, is a volcano challenge. Etna is the largest volcano in Europe and one of the tallest in the world. It is also one of the most active. Etna has been erupting almost continually for close to half a million years. It has the nickname "The Friendly Giant" because very few of its eruptions have resulted in death since people began keeping records of its activity in 1500 B.C. Scientists at Italy's volcano-tracking agency believe that this may change because Etna's eruptions are becoming more frequent with more magma building up at the volcano's core. Since Italian volcanologists are watching Etna closely, it is likely that they will be able to warn residents near the volcano when a serious eruption is about to happen.

Kinds of eruptions

Volcanologists study volcanoes from several observatories located all over the world. They watch lava flows and measure ground movements. Volcanologists categorize volcanoes and eruptions.

How big?

Volcanologists measure and compare the force of one volcano eruption to another using a rating system called the Volcano Explosivity Index (VEI). They measure how much rock, lava, and ash is expelled during an eruption and how far rock fragments are shot out by the volcano. They also measure the height of the giant cloud of dust that explodes from the volcano upon eruption. The VEI rating system gives each eruption a score from zero to eight. Volcanoes with a VEI rating of zero are non-explosive and mild. A VEI rated eruption of eight is considered "mega-colossal" and has not occured on Earth for thousands of years.

Eruption behavior

Volcanologists label eruptions according to a "pattern of behavior". Some volcanoes show several of these patterns in one eruption. A Hawaiian eruption occurs along fissures, or on a central vent, where lava spews and collects in flows or pools. In a Vesuvian eruption, named after the volcano Vesuvius in Italy, ash and gas spew up and rain down several miles from the volcano. Other types of eruption include the most powerful, Plinian, as well as Pelean, Strombolian, Volcanian, and Phreatic.

Volcano types

There are five main types of volcanoes: stratovolcano, caldera , shield, cinder cone, and lava dome. A stratovolcano, or composite volcano, has steep sides and is usually topped by a crater. Stratovolcanoes are built up from layers of ash, lava, and debris. When lava cools near the top of a volcanic vent and blocks it, violent explosions that follow can blow the entire top off the volcano, leaving a huge opening. Volcanoes formed this way are called caldera volcanoes. Shield volcanoes are shield shaped and formed by lava. Lava dome volcanoes are formed when lava pours over the side of a volcano's vent and forms dome-like walls. Cinder cone volcanoes happen when lava spews from a central vent to form a cone.

Cowpat volcanic bombs are pieces of lava thrown out during a violent volcanic eruption.

Volcanic ribbon bombs are formed when streamers of lava harden in mid-air.

A volcanic steam ring made when steam was ejected from a round volcanic vent on Mount Etna in Italy.

Blowing their tops

Hawaiian eruption: lava arcs from fissures or a central vent and sometimes collects in a lake or cone.

Strombolian eruption: A burst of lava with rocks and bombs.

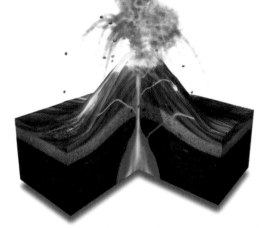

Vesuvian: gas and ash blow from a cauliflower shaped cloud above the volcano.

Pelean eruption: cloud of gas, ash, and dust glow above volcano while streams of lava run down the sides.

Famous volcanoes

Every year, volcanoes erupt all over the world. Some erupt frequently, with so little violence, that the people who live near them see them as simple facts of life. Throughout history, there have been several volcanic eruptions that have been anything but ordinary.

Some volcanic eruptions have been so devastating that they have killed more than 30,000 people – about the size of an entire North American town. Imagine a town of this size today, completely wiped off the map, with all of its **inhabitants** killed as well, and you will have an idea of the devastation caused by some of history's deadliest volcanoes.

Krakatoa

In 1883, the world's most famous volcanic island, called Krakatoa, erupted. Located in Indonesia, Krakatoa's explosion was reportedly heard more than 3000 miles (5000 km) away in Australia. Ash from the explosion darkened skies as far away as New York and London, and Krakatoa's eruption destroyed more than 60 percent of the uninhabited island, and caused a huge **tsunami** that crashed into the nearby islands of Java and Sumatra, killing more than 36,000 people.

A newspaper from September 1883 shows how Krakatoa "blew up".

Vesuvius 79 A.D.

Vesuvius

One of the world's best-known volcanoes is famous not because of the destruction caused by its tragic eruption in 79 A.D., but because of what it left behind. Today, if you visit the historic sites at the cities of Pompeii and Herculaneum in Italy, you can see some of the results of the eruption of Mount Vesuvius. Vesuvius was **dormant** for 800 years before it erupted, killing more than 2000 people and burying the entire town in more than 15 feet (5 meters) of ash. The people in the cities were caught unaware. Most were **suffocated** by the ash. So much ash was deposited on the two towns, bodies of people and animals trying to escape left inpressions in the ash when it hardened. Almost 2000 years later, scientists made plaster casts of the mummified impressions that revealed the figures of those who lived there and how they died.

The bodies of people killed at Pompeii were preserved as they died by the volcanic ash.

Mt. Pelée

For several days in 1902, clouds of smoke and ash spewed from the mountain, but the residents of the sleepy village of St. Pierre on the Caribbean island of Martinique ignored it. Government officials inspected the volcano and declared it safe. They did not want people to leave their homes, particularly as an election was soon to be held. Mt. Pelée erupted May 5, with searing clouds of gas and choking dust. The deadly stream of volcanic matter then sped along the ground and into the city where it smashed and burned everything in its path – walls, buildings, streets and, worst of all, about 30,000 people. Amazingly, two people survived. One survivor was a prisoner locked in an underground cell whose life was saved because he had been forced to stay beneath the path of Mount Pelée's deadly stream of hot rock, ash, and gas.

1902

Mt. Pelée 1902

Mt. Pelée's eruption sent a searing pyroclastic flow down the volcano and into the streets of St. Pierre.

Mt. Pinatubo 1991

In April 1991, Mount Pinatubo, in the Philippines, began a 10-week-long series of eruptions that sent tons of ash and pumice into the air. Almost 1000 people died as a result of Pinatubo's eruption. Thousands more were evacuated.

Montserrat

Thousands of people fled volcanic eruptions on the West Indian island of Montserrat in the 1990s. Pyroclastic flows of debris endngered island towns in the volcano's path.

An island is born

In 1963, an underwater volcano created a new island in the North Atlantic Ocean. The volcano's eruption caused water to become hot and a giant plume of smoke shot up from under the surface. Nearby fishermen thought they were seeing a ship on fire. In reality, the new island, named Surtsey, in honor of Surtur, the Norse god of fire was created. The lava that emerged from the volcano hardened, creating the base of the island and several later eruptions during the next four years added more and more height to the island, until it had risen nearly 600 feet (180 m) above sea level.

Sturtsey emerges from the ocean.

Staying Safe

Most cities and towns near active volcanoes have some sort of emergency plan in place for when eruptions occur. Residents live with the knowledge that if the volcano erupts, they may have to leave quickly.

Volcanic ash fills a yard in a village in Iceland.

(bottom) What looks like the result of a violent storm is actually volcano damage from a mud flow.

Staying safe

Organizations that lend disaster assistance, such as the **Red Cross** or **Red Crescent**, advise that people who live near volcanoes prepare evacuation plans. By making an escape plan in advance, people can know what to do and react more quickly when faced with an emergency.

Volcanic ash creates a fog in a Costa Rican town 20 miles (32 kilometers) from the volcano.

Set up a plan

Minimize your risk by making and following survival plans

- Map out an evacuation plan and a back up plan if the original route is blocked.
- Assign a family friend or relative to act as a contact person during an emergency. The contact person's name, address, and phone number should be memorized.
- The Red Cross recommends that the contact person be someone who lives outside the area.

Emergency supplies

Knowing how you will live through a disaster is the first step.

- Have a flashlight and extra batteries on hand in case of a power outage.
- Put together a disaster kit with supplies such as bottled water, a transistor radio, non-perishable food supplies, and a first aid kit.
- Put several dust masks in the disaster kit along with long-sleeve shirts and goggles for every member of the family in case of ashfall. Keep the family car and other engines turned off if ash is falling.
- If trapped indoors during an eruption, close all windows, doors and dampers. Bring all animals under cover.
- Follow the evacuation orders issued by local authorities and keep clear of areas down wind and down river valleys from a volcano.

After the volcano

Even after a volcanic eruption is over, there can still be great danger. Large amounts of volcanic ash that is present in the air can make it difficult to breathe.

Large eruptions can have a huge effect on the local and world environments. After the powerful eruption of Mount Pinatubo in 1991, huge amounts of **sulfuric acid particles** that had been expelled into the air were caught up in winds and spread around the Earth's atmosphere. This created a layer of thick cloud that blocked sunlight and dropped the world's temperature by almost one degree during the next two years. The change in temperature, lack of sunlight and increase in harmful chemicals in the air after a violent eruption, effects livestock and crop growth.

(above) Filipino volunteers clean volcanic ash spewed by Mount Pinatubo from the streets while shielding their noses and mouths with homemade masks. Ash makes it difficult to breathe.

Heavy as ash

Volcanic ash, or tephra, is another danger. The heavy ash collects on the roofs of buildings causing them to collapse if not cleared off. Ash is **abrasive** and makes it difficult to operate vehicles because it clogs engines and damages sensitive equipment. Clogging also effects airplanes in flight, making it impossible for planes to fly safely near erupting volcanoes.

Lahars, or volcanic mudflows, can destroy houses and roads with swift flowing debris.

Clearing debris

Cleanup efforts also mean breaking up hardened magma in order to restore roads; removing debris such as broken buildings, downed trees and crumbled bridges; and even the recovery of people killed during the eruption. The cleanup can be dangerous. In 2002, residents of the capital city of Quito, Ecuador, were left with the task of removing one million tons of ash deposited on city roofs and roads after the eruption of the Reventador volcano. One person was killed and 16 were seriously hurt as they slipped off rooftops during cleanup efforts.

Under the volcano

People living in areas near active volcanoes need forecasts to help them plan their daily lives. Many volcanoes erupt mildly on a regular basis, such as those in Hawaii or Iceland. Living near a volcano means managing the risks.

Saving a town

The fishing village of Vestmannaeyjar on the island of Heimaey in Iceland was nearly destroyed in 1973 after the Eldfell volcano erupted. Eldfell, which means "fire mountain" in Icelandic, began erupting in the middle of the night. About 5,000 residents of the village were evacuated by fishing trawlers when the volcano began spewing pyroclastic bombs and ash. Several hundred volunteers stayed behind for five months to battle the volcano. They fought the lava flow by spraying nearly six million tons of seawater at it. The water, from 43 pumps, saved the town's fishing port and processing plants. By the time residents came back to live in Heimaey, $100 million had been spent fighting the volcano and rebuilding lost homes and businesses.

Houses in Vestmannaeyjar covered with volcanic ash. Volunteers cleared roofs, and fought an advancing column of lava to save the town and its fishing port.

(above) Mudpools bubble with volcanic heat. In some parts of the world, the heat from volcanoes can be turned into geothermal energy used to heat homes.

(left) Soil that has been enriched by volcanic ash and other materials is very fertile.

Rating a volcano

There are only about 60 significant volcano eruptions a year. If a volcano erupts daily, it is assigned a Volcanic Explosivity Index (VEI) rating of zero to one. A rating of two, means that the volcano produces about 1.3 million cubic yards (1 million cubic meters) of rock fragments when it erupts. A VEI-3 eruption, however, is ten times worse. Depending on the environmental conditions, even a volcano with a "low" score can be dangerous. The Nevado del Ruiz eruption in Colombia in 1985 had a VEI rating of "only" three, but it killed 23,000 people.

Living near a volcano means living with a the risk that the volcano will erupt and destroy property and threaten lives.

Recipe for Disaster

In this well-known activity, a mixture of water and baking soda act as the magma for your volcano. It is up to you to construct the volcano walls in a way that will allow the eruption to occur – just like a real volcano.

What you need:

*Baking Soda
*Vinegar
*A small jar or plastic container
*Plaster of Paris (To build your volcano walls)
*Paper towels for volcano cleanup

** Make sure an adult is present during the experiment.

What to do:

1. Use the plaster of Paris to form your volcano. (You can also use clay, modeling clay or even soil, if you can find a way to get it to hold together.) Make the volcano opening big enough to fit your jar or plastic container.

2. Pour some vinegar into the jar, and place it into the center of the volcano.

3. Add the baking soda, and stand back! There will be lots of fizzing, popping, and bubbling during the "eruption".

4. Observe what happens, and ask an adult to take a picture during the "eruption".

What you will see:

Your volcano will erupt and bubble and spill over the sides, just like a real volcano.

Glossary

abrasive something that is harsh or scraping.

Andes Mountains a mountain range in western South America that contains several volcanoes.

basalt a hard, glassy, dark, volcanic rock.

blacksmith someone who forges, or shapes iron with a hammer.

convection the upward movement of air that has been heated.

dormant asleep or temporarily inactive or quiet.

fissures long narrow openings or cracks.

Himalyan Range a mountain range in south central Asia.

inhabitants residents or people who live in an area.

non-perishible food that does not spoil or rot, such as canned goods.

pyroclastic volcanic cloud composed mostly of rock fragments.

Red Cross/Red Crescent an international organization that cares for people sick, wounded, or homeless by wars or disasters.

suffocated killed by blocking access to air.

sulfuric acid particles tiny droplets of a corrosive oily liquid.

tsunami a large ocean wave caused by an underwater earthquake or volcanic eruption.

Index

2 3 4 5 6 7 8 9 0 Printed in the U.S.A. 3 2 1 0 9 8 7 6 5